INTRODUCTION

Although each princess in this book is unique, they all have something in common: They spend a lot of time helping others. They use their voices and talents to make their communities safer, stronger, and healthier. They are creative in the ways they approach challenges, and they are problem solvers.

Princesses—like us—have big futures ahead, and their lives—like ours—are changing all the time. They may become involved in new projects, and their dreams may look a bit different tomorrow than they do today.

Even so, each princess shows how one person can work hard to make small changes, and those changes can add up to a better world!

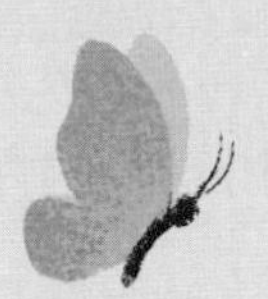

To all the women in this book—and beyond—who live their ideals.
And to Kelly Sonnack, the Princess of Patience, who sees diamonds within the cobblestones.

—C. A. P.

For my mom, who always treats us like little princesses.

—D. H.

Published by Roaring Brook Press
Roaring Brook Press is a division of Holtzbrinck Publishing Holdings Limited Partnership
120 Broadway, New York, NY 10271 • mackids.com

Library of Congress Control Number: 2022910305

First edition, 2023 • Book design by Mina Chung
Printed in China by RR Donnelley Asia Printing Solutions Ltd., Dongguan City, Guangdong Province

ISBN 978-1-250-75143-0
1 3 5 7 9 10 8 6 4 2

REAL PRINCESSES CHANGE THE WORLD

CARRIE A. PEARSON

Illustrated by DUNG HO

ROARING BROOK PRESS

NEW YORK

TABLE OF CONTENTS

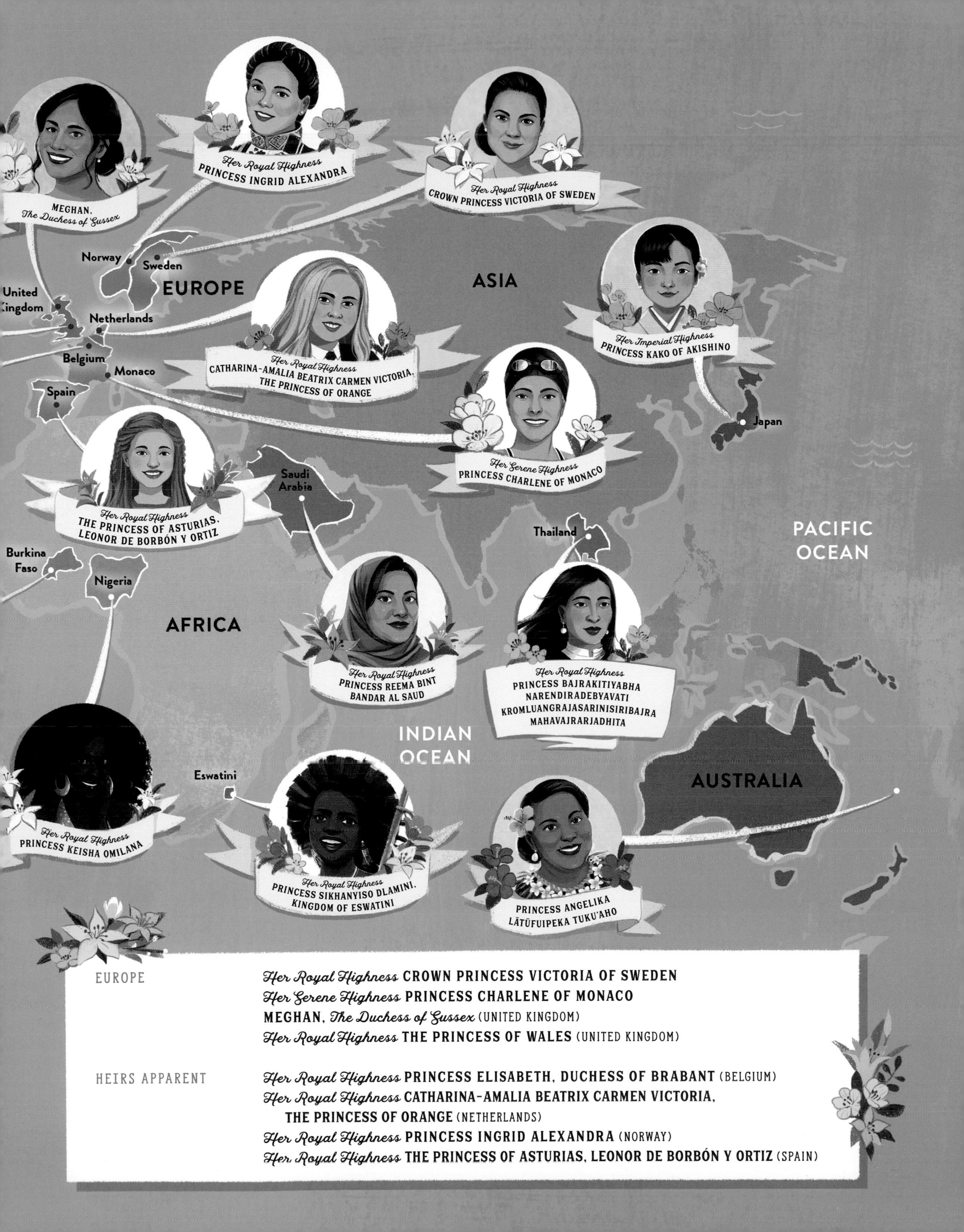

EUROPE

Her Royal Highness **CROWN PRINCESS VICTORIA OF SWEDEN**
Her Serene Highness **PRINCESS CHARLENE OF MONACO**
MEGHAN, *The Duchess of Sussex* (UNITED KINGDOM)
Her Royal Highness **THE PRINCESS OF WALES** (UNITED KINGDOM)

HEIRS APPARENT

Her Royal Highness **PRINCESS ELISABETH, DUCHESS OF BRABANT** (BELGIUM)
Her Royal Highness **CATHARINA-AMALIA BEATRIX CARMEN VICTORIA, THE PRINCESS OF ORANGE** (NETHERLANDS)
Her Royal Highness **PRINCESS INGRID ALEXANDRA** (NORWAY)
Her Royal Highness **THE PRINCESS OF ASTURIAS, LEONOR DE BORBÓN Y ORTIZ** (SPAIN)

Her Royal Highness

PRINCESS ABZE DJIGMA

BURKINA FASO, AFRICA

Real princesses are ENGINEERS.

When Princess Abze Djigma was a little girl, she and her family had only one light source—kerosene lamps that were smoky, smelly, and dangerous. It was hard to read or study, but Princess Abze wanted to learn. Her parents sent her to school in England, where better light and opportunity existed.

Princess Abze became an engineer, but she never forgot how hard it was to learn when she was younger. So, she created a small, solar-powered light for families who don't have electricity in their homes. Called MAMA-LIGHT, it recharges easily, doesn't cost much, and illuminates for hours.

For those with access to electricity, it may seem easy to turn on a lamp when they need it. But nearly a billion people in the world today do not have electricity. Princess Abze's MAMA-LIGHT helps many learn, be safer, and even run their businesses.

Futures are brighter because of Princess Abze.

Her Royal Highness

PRINCESS SIKHANYISO DLAMINI, KINGDOM OF ESWATINI

ESWATINI, AFRICA

Real princesses are **COMPUTER EXPERTS.**

When Princess Sikhanyiso was just seven years old, her father, the king, gave her two important responsibilities. She became Chief Maiden for the Kingdom of Eswatini, and she led the yearly Umhlanga Reed Dance. At this celebration, thousands of girls and young women gather to learn from one another, perform traditional dances, and express their love for His Majesty the King and Her Majesty the Queen Mother.

Princess Sikhanyiso held these roles for twenty years.

But her life wasn't all dances and ceremonies; she also attended schools in three countries and earned a master's degree in digital communication.

Now her job is to manage how her country uses computers and other technology. She creates connections between people and businesses to build a stronger nation.

As Princess Sikhanyiso said, "The sky is the limit in the Kingdom of Eswatini." She helps her country reach for it.

Her Royal Highness

PRINCESS KEISHA OMILANA

NIGERIA, AFRICA

Real princesses are **BUSINESSWOMEN.**

Keisha Bolden was born in California, USA. Later, she became a fashion designer, actor, and model. Keisha broke many barriers in these fields by wearing her hair naturally.

When Keisha married Prince Adekunle Adebayo Omilana of the Arigbabuwo royal family in Nigeria, she became a princess. They live in London and have two children together.

Today, Princess Keisha still models and acts, but she's also a public speaker, educator, and business owner. Through her self-created business, A Crown of Curls, Princess Keisha teaches parents how to care for their children's hair—especially if it is a different texture or type than their own.

Princess Keisha shows children that their hair is beautiful and, most importantly, that *they* are beautiful. She encourages children to love themselves because when they do, they can break barriers, too.

CROWN of Curls

Her Imperial Highness

PRINCESS KAKO OF AKISHINO

JAPAN, ASIA

Real princesses are DEDICATED.

Princess Kako was born into the world's oldest continuous family monarchy. The Imperial Family of Japan dates back at least fifteen hundred years! She grew up surrounded by its rich history and traditions.

After graduating from college, Princess Kako stepped into her obligations and now devotes her life to her country and monarchy. She represents Japan at ceremonies and in formal meetings at home and around the world.

Princess Kako said, "It is not about what I want to do, but about addressing the official duties that have been asked of me." She chose to follow a path of service to the Imperial Family of Japan.

Her Royal Highness

PRINCESS REEMA BINT BANDAR AL SAUD

SAUDI ARABIA, ASIA

Real princesses are VISIONARIES.

In 2017, Princess Reema stepped into a unique and important job in Saudi Arabia: encouraging businesses, schools, and local communities to allow women and girls to be involved in sports.

She gave speeches, held meetings with officials, and spoke one-on-one with people to help them see how this change would benefit girls—and everyone in the country, too.

Now girls in every public school take gym classes. Women can own fitness centers and play sports. Several stadiums in Saudi Arabia give access to women so they can watch games that men play. Saudi women who only dreamed of competing in the Olympics can train and represent their country.

Because of Princess Reema and others who share her vision, women and girls in Saudi Arabia have more opportunities than ever before.

Her Royal Highness

PRINCESS BAJRAKITIYABHA NARENDIRADEBYAVATI KROMLUANGRAJASARINISIRIBAJRA MAHAVAJRARJADHITA

THAILAND, ASIA

Real princesses are **LAWYERS.**

When Princess Bajrakitiyabha was young, she attended one of the first girls'-only schools in Thailand—a school started by her great-grandmother, Queen Saovabha Phongsri. The princess went on to earn four college degrees in liberal arts and law, including a doctorate of juridical science.

Princess Bajarkitiyabha realized that many Thai women struggled to earn money legally, which led to them being imprisoned. So, she started the Nabha Foundation to teach jailed Thai women how to make products like food and beauty-care items. Once they are released from prison, these women can make and sell the items to support themselves and their families.

In addition to supporting Thai women, Princess Bajrakitiyabha speaks up for female prisoners around the world. She helped create the Bangkok Rules, adopted by the United Nations, hoping that imprisoned women in every country would be treated properly.

As a lawyer, Princess Bajrakitiyabha acts on behalf of women everywhere.

PRINCESS ANGELIKA LĀTŪFUIPEKA TUKU'AHO

TONGA, AUSTRALIA/OCEANIA

Real princesses are AMBASSADORS.

An ambassador is like a human bridge connecting one place to another. Princess Lātūfuipeka is this bridge for Tonga.

She is the first woman to be appointed as a Tongan ambassador, known as a High Commissioner in her country. She hosts gatherings for officials and visiting royalty where Tongans dance, sing, and share their customs. These activities teach visitors about the unique Tongan culture.

Princess Lātūfuipeka also connects the Tongan people with their own culture. She inspires them to practice their traditional dances, songs, and art. She reminds the women in her community that their legacy skills, like weaving *ta'ovala* (a mat worn around the waist), can give them opportunities today. Thanks in part to Princess Lātūfuipeka's efforts, beautiful *ta'ovala* and original artwork are in demand by visitors from other countries.

Princess Lātūfuipeka is connecting the past with the present—and Tonga with the world.

Her Royal Highness

CROWN PRINCESS VICTORIA OF SWEDEN

SWEDEN, EUROPE

Real princesses are ENVIRONMENTALISTS.

Crown Princess Victoria of Sweden wanted to protect the environment. But first, she needed to understand the reasons why it was in danger.

So, she sailed on ships with scientists studying the climate crisis. She visited research stations in the Arctic and helped sample the ice to look for changes over time. She realized that one behavior, like overfishing in the ocean, can hurt something else, like the sea creatures that depend on fish to survive.

The Crown Princess continues to learn from environmental experts. She shares their work with leaders of countries and businesses, asking them to respect and protect our planet and our water.

The Crown Princess once said, "Climate change and air pollution are concrete problems, and we need to act now." Thankfully, in her role as the future Queen of Sweden, she will have even more opportunities to protect our planet.

Her Serene Highness

PRINCESS CHARLENE OF MONACO

MONACO, EUROPE

Real princesses are ATHLETES.

Because her mother was a swimming instructor, Charlene Wittstock first jumped into a pool when she was a very young child. Later, Charlene began swimming competitively and represented her home country of South Africa in the 2000 Olympics.

A few years after the Olympics, she married Prince Albert of Monaco and became a princess. Today she lives with her family in a country nestled by the Mediterranean Sea.

Princess Charlene still loves swimming, although she knows water can be dangerous, too. Her mission is to save lives worldwide by funding swimming lessons, speaking up about water safety, and teaching rescue techniques.

Thanks to Princess Charlene, many more children can safely splash, swim, and enjoy the water. They might even become champion swimmers themselves.

MEGHAN,

The Duchess of Sussex

UNITED KINGDOM, EUROPE

Real princesses are FEMINISTS.

Meghan Markle was born in California. When she was eleven years old, she saw a commercial on TV about washing dishes—and it was aimed only at women. Meghan wrote a letter to the company, speaking up for women and girls, and the company changed its commercial shortly after.

Meghan built a successful career as an actor and eventually married Prince Harry, The Duke of Sussex. The Duchess and The Duke of Sussex are no longer working members of the royal family. However, The Duchess of Sussex continues to speak up for women with her words and actions and through the organizations she supports.

One group provides guidance for women who are looking for jobs. Another assists women who feed their hungry neighbors. And another provides mental health resources to Black women and girls.

Meghan, The Duchess of Sussex, is a feminist. She's working toward a world where, no matter their gender, all people are treated equally and with compassion.

thank
you

Her Royal Highness

THE PRINCESS OF WALES

UNITED KINGDOM, EUROPE

Real princesses SPEAK UP FOR CHILDREN.

The Princess of Wales is helping adults understand how important childhood is.

When Catherine Middleton married Prince William, The Duke of Cambridge, she became a duchess and later, Princess of Wales. She knew that healthy, happy children more often grow up to be healthy, happy adults. But, she wondered, did people understand how much childhood impacts who a person becomes as an adult?

She decided to ask. The Princess and other experts created a survey called "5 Big Questions on the Under Fives" and shared it with people in her country. Almost half a million people completed the questionnaire! Surprisingly, most of them did not realize how vital it is to have a positive childhood.

Now the project team can work on fixing problems found through the survey. Children's lives will be better today, and they will become even stronger and more capable tomorrow.

The Princess of Wales speaks up for children because she believes that "big change starts small."

Real princesses are LEARNING TO BE LEADERS.

These four princesses are *heirs apparent*—next in line to lead their monarchies as queens.

In many monarchies worldwide, the rules about who can be the next heir apparent are changing. Now, in these monarchies, the firstborn child of the current king or queen, no matter their gender, can lead. In Norway, Princess Ingrid is the first female heir apparent in over six hundred years. Princess Leonor is the first in more than 150 years. Princess Elisabeth will be the first female leader of the Belgium monarchy in history.

Getting ready for this role is a lot of work! The princesses go to school or college full time, sometimes living away from home. They study different languages—often three or more—to better understand those from other nations. They practice meeting people outside their family and listening to their concerns.

The princesses represent their countries at special events, sometimes wearing traditional clothing. They learn to behave in ways that honor their monarchy. In speeches they write and give, the princesses offer their hopes for their communities—and the world.

Each day, these princesses discover that becoming a good leader takes time and preparation. Much like you, they are growing into all they can be and do.

Her Royal Highness
CATHARINA-AMALIA
BEATRIX CARMEN
VICTORIA,
THE PRINCESS OF
ORANGE
(NETHERLANDS, EUROPE)
(B. 2003)
Her Royal Highness
THE PRINCESS
OF ASTURIAS,
LEONOR
DE BORBÓN Y ORTIZ
(SPAIN, EUROPE)
(B. 2005)
Her Royal Highness
PRINCESS ELISABETH,
DUCHESS OF
BRABANT
(BELGIUM, EUROPE)
(B. 2001)
Her Royal Highness
PRINCESS INGRID
ALEXANDRA
(NORWAY, EUROPE)
(B. 2004)

AUTHOR'S NOTE

Once upon a time, there was a mom with three daughters who loved pretending to be princesses. They danced in princess costumes, watched princess movies, and played with princess-y toys. Although the daughters had fun, the mother felt frustrated that she couldn't find books to share about real princesses. She wanted her daughters to learn how women in royal families spent their days—probably not always wearing long sparkly dresses or going to balls—and how they used their roles to make the world better.

The daughters grew up and stopped playing princess. But the mother never forgot about wanting real princess stories to share. By this time, the mother was a children's book author, and she decided to ask other children what they thought about princesses. Many years had passed, and the internet provided more ways to learn about royal families. Surprisingly, children still thought princesses were more like the fairy-tale version than real life.

The time had come for the mother (me!) to research real princesses. Just as I suspected, princesses use their skills and ambitions to make the world better. Now I can share this information with my daughters and children everywhere. *Real Princesses Change the World* is the book I wished we'd had.

The End.

GLOSSARY

CROWN PRINCESS OR CROWN PRINCE: The next person to lead the monarchy, or the wife of a crown prince or husband of a crown princess.

MONARCHY AND MONARCH: A monarchy is a form of government led by a single person known as a monarch. Monarchs use titles such as king, queen, emperor, or empress. Usually, monarchs stay in their role their whole lives unless they decide to leave the monarchy. Then the next person in line (often a son or brother, sometimes a daughter) steps into the role.

PRINCESS AND DUCHESS: In the British monarchy, females born into a royal family use the title of princess. A non-royal who marries a duke is called a duchess. Not all monarchies use this distinction.

ROYALTY: A person or group of people in the monarchy.

STYLE: A legal or official name for a member of royalty such as "Her Royal Highness" (also shown as "HRH").

WHO SAID IT?

MATCH EACH QUOTE WITH THE PRINCESS WHO SAID IT!

1. *"Social harmony will only be achieved when everybody realizes their own rights without violating the rights of others."*

2. *"We can be engineers, and we can be female."*

3. *"It is our duty . . . to give all children the space to build their emotional strength and provide a strong foundation for their future."*

4. *"A better-connected Eswatini will translate into a more prosperous Eswatini."*

5. *"The world is so big—and at the same time so amazingly small. Everything is connected in a complex and fragile interaction. If we only look at one part, we miss out on the big picture."*

6. *"Our dances show the proud history of our past, preserving our values for our present generation and ensuring a promising future for our generations to come."*

7. *“I do have dreams, but I prefer to keep them to myself.”*

8. *“I LOVE receiving checks . . . with my name on them.”*

9. *“It is equally important for me to be with my children as to reach many children, to help them, to educate them, to make a difference for them, and to save their lives.”*

10. *"If things are wrong and there is a lack of justice and an inequality, someone needs to say something—and why can’t it be you?”*

11. *“It’s not about being the first; it’s about being one of the many to come.”*

ANSWERS TO “WHO SAID IT?”

1. Princess Bajrakitiyabha of Thailand
2. Princess Abze Djigma of Burkina Faso
3. The Princess of Wales, United Kingdom
4. Princess Sikhanyiso Dlamini of Eswatini
5. Crown Princess Victoria of Sweden
6. Princess Lātūfuipeka of Tonga
7. Princess Kako of Japan
8. Princess Keisha Omilana of Nigeria
9. Princess Charlene of Monaco
10. Meghan, The Duchess of Sussex, United Kingdom
11. Princess Reema of Saudi Arabia

DREAM BIG QUESTIONS

- If you were a lawyer like Princess Bajrakitiyabha, what laws would you make?
- If you were an engineer like Princess Abze, what would you design?
- If you wanted to speak up for children like The Princess of Wales, how would you help young people?
- If you were a computer expert like Princess Sikhanyiso, how would you use technology to help your country?
- If you were an environmentalist like Crown Princess Victoria of Sweden, what changes would you make to protect our earth?
- If you were an ambassador like Princess Lātūfuipeka, how would you share your culture?
- If you were dedicated like Princess Kako, what things would you do for your family?
- If you were a businesswoman like Princess Keisha, what company would you like to start?
- If you were an athlete like Princess Charlene of Monaco, what would your sport be?
- If you were a feminist like Meghan, The Duchess of Sussex, how would you make the world more equal for all?
- If you were a visionary like Princess Reema, what would you change?
- If you were an heir apparent like Princesses Elisabeth, Catharina-Amalia, Ingrid Alexandra, and Leonor, how would you prepare to be a leader?

FURTHER INFORMATION

Her Royal Highness Princess Abze Djigma (Burkina Faso): princess-abze.org/about-h-r-h-princess-abze-djigma

Her Royal Highness Princess Sikhanyiso Dlamini, Kingdom of Eswatini: linkedin.com/in/ziondlamini/?originalSubdomain=sz

Her Royal Highness Princess Keisha Omilana (Nigeria): acrownofcurls.com

Her Imperial Highness Princess Kako of Akishino (Japan): kunaicho.go.jp/e-about/

Her Royal Highness Princess Reema bint Bandar Al Saud (Saudi Arabia): saudiembassy.net/ambassador

Her Royal Highness Princess Bajrakitiyabha Narendiradebyavati Kromluangrajasarinisiribajra Mahavajrarjadhita (Thailand): nabha.or.th/eng_version.html

Princess Angelika Lātūfuipeka Tuku'aho (Tonga): tongahighcom.com.au

Her Royal Highness Crown Princess Victoria of Sweden: kungahuset.se/royalcourt/royalfamily/hrhcrownprincessvictoria.4.396160511584257f218000503.html

Her Serene Highness Princess Charlene of Monaco: palais.mc/en/princely-family/h-s-h-princess-charlene/biography-1-6.html

Meghan, The Duchess of Sussex (United Kingdom): royal.uk/duchess-sussex

Her Royal Highness The Princess of Wales (United Kingdom): royal.uk/the-princess-of-wales

Her Royal Highness Princess Elisabeth, Duchess of Brabant (Belgium): monarchie.be/en/royal-family/princess-elisabeth-duchess-of-brabant

Her Royal Highness Princess Ingrid Alexandra (Norway): royalcourt.no/artikkel.html?tid=28778&sek=28633

Her Royal Highness Catharina-Amalia Beatrix Carmen Victoria, the Princess of Orange (Netherlands): royal-house.nl/members-royal-house/the-princess-of-orange

Her Royal Highness the Princess of Asturias, Leonor de Borbón y Ortiz (Spain): casareal.es/ES/FamiliaReal/PrincesaLeonor/Paginas/subhome.aspx

CROWN
Curls
CROWN
Curls
CROWN
Curls